The *Romantic* *Spirit*
1790–1910

Selected, edited and annotated by Nancy Bachus

21 Intermediate to Early Advanced Piano Solos
Reflecting the Influence of 13 Great Composers on the Romantic Period

Alfred

Cover art: *Frédéric Chopin in the Salon of the Prince Anton Radziwill*
by Henryk Siemiradzki (1843–1902)
AKG Photo, London

oreword by Fernando Laires

Nancy Bachus's *The Romantic Spirit* is brilliantly conceived for both the present and the future. The new century will inevitably bring new ways of life and educational values that will challenge piano teachers to reevaluate the purposes and orientation of their teaching. While music will remain essential to human beings and to the education of the young, new teaching ideas will be needed to adapt to the future dynamics of our changing society.

Illustrated with historical paintings and quotations, and containing information about composers, the style of their works and the mechanism of the piano, *The Romantic Spirit* meets this challenge by showing students music's relationship with literary, scientific, social and political events. This integration of music with other fields of knowledge broadens the scope of their education, and promotes greater interest in continuing piano studies.

The pieces are of contrasting moods, tempos, forms, styles and piano techniques. The music is sure to spark students' interest as the pieces are engaging to learn and perform. Because of the special educational value of *The Romantic Spirit* and also because it is advisable for students to learn works above and below their current level, the music in *The Romantic Spirit*, Books 1 and 2 may be studied in any order.

The Romantic Spirit is certain to be an indispensable resource for every piano teacher and student.

Fernando Laires has successfully combined an international career as concert pianist, recording artist and teacher. For his debut in Lisbon, Portugal, at age 19, he performed all 32 Beethoven piano sonatas in a series of 10 recitals. Mr. Laires has held artist faculty positions at various institutions in Europe, the United States and in China. He is co-founder and current president of the American Liszt Society. In addition, he has served on the juries of many international piano competitions, including the Tchaikovsky in Moscow and the Van Cliburn in Texas.

reface by Nancy Bachus

To understand and interpret musical style one must recapture the spirit of the environment in which composers lived, created and performed. Romantic music developed in 19th-century Europe when musicians were frequently writers, painters, philosophers and historians as well as masters of their musical art. *The Romantic Spirit* comes alive by integrating historical information and artwork with the piano pieces written during this period. Knowledge of the great attainments and heritage of our Western civilization fosters a deeper and more personal lifelong experience with the great art of piano playing.

Nancy Bachus is a graduate of the Eastman School of Music where she studied with pianist Eugene List and accompanist Brooks Smith. Her articles have been published in various keyboard magazines. Nancy has taught over 25 years at the college and university levels as well as at the National Music Camp at Interlochen, Michigan. Certified as a Master Teacher by the Music Teachers National Association (MTNA), Nancy currently maintains an independent piano studio in Hudson, Ohio. A teacher and recitalist, she has been a featured clinician for numerous piano teachers' organizations and music conventions.

Contents

Ludwig van Beethoven (1770–1827)

"Keep an eye on this boy [Beethoven]. Someday he will force the world to talk about him."

Wolfgang Amadeus Mozart (1756–1791)[1]

"There was a certain magic in the expression [of his piano playing]. ... Frequently there was not a single dry eye, and many [listeners] broke out in loud sobs."

Carl Czerny (1791–1857), Austrian pianist, teacher, composer and pupil of Beethoven[2]

Ludwig van Beethoven

© Planet Art

The Beginnings of Romanticism

Beethoven wrote predominately in Classical forms, such as sonatas and symphonies, but Romantic elements were present.

- ▪ He believed in the "revolutionary" ideal of the equality, freedom and dignity of man.

- ▪ He viewed music as a moral force that could influence human character.

- ▪ Nature served as musical inspiration and healer for his soul.

- ▪ His personal struggles and his overwhelming emotions are expressed in his music.

- ▪ He created the first character pieces, the *Bagatelles,* for piano.

His compositions and piano playing made him well known and accepted in Viennese society. In spite of his bad disposition and poor manners, leading aristocrats, recognizing his genius, welcomed him into their salons.

Austrian Princes Lobkowitz and Kinsky and Archduke Rudolph signed a pact in 1809 granting Beethoven a lifetime salary so that he could remain in Vienna and be free to compose.

[1]Philippe A. Autexier, *Beethoven, the Composer as Hero* (New York: Harry N. Abrams, Inc., 1992), 23.

[2]F. V. Grunfeld, *Age of Revolution* (New York: Time, Inc., 1968), 20.

For many years this was accepted as the last piano piece written by Beethoven.
Today some scholars say that was a "romantic" tale, and he did not write this piece.

Farewell to the Piano

Attributed to
Ludwig van Beethoven
(1770–1827)

Moderato con molto espressione

(a) The Editor suggests the chord be rolled before the beat so the left-hand G-sharp is played exactly
with the right-hand C-sharp on beat 1. This applies to all rolled chords in this collection.

(b) The Editor suggests that grace notes begin before the beat.

One of the most popular 19th-century ballroom dances,
the **waltz** was associated with Vienna.

Gertrude's Waltz

Ludwig van Beethoven
(1770–1827)

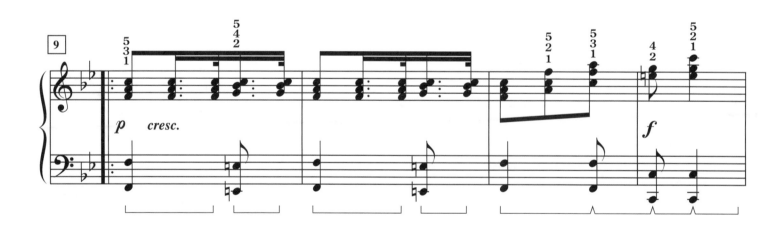

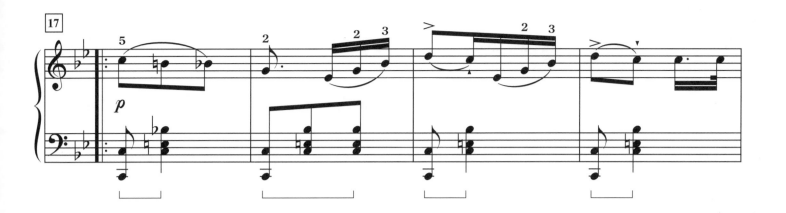

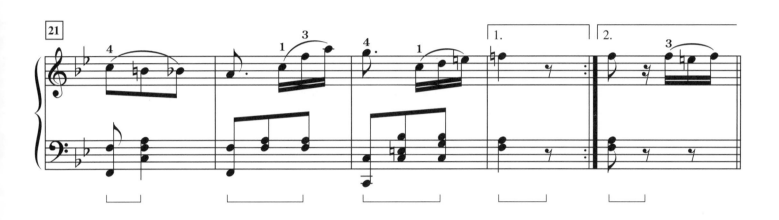

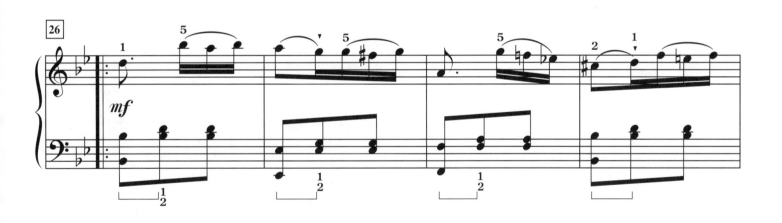

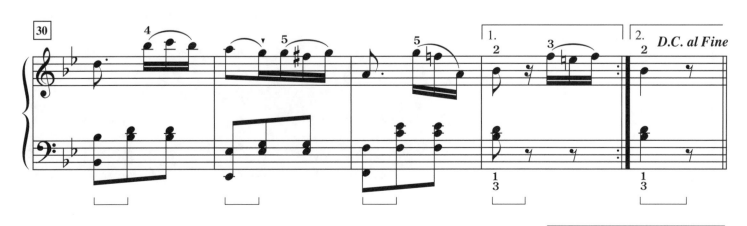

The Age of Romanticism (1790–1910)

Romantic composers wanted music to sound the way emotions felt: heart over head, instinct over reason, and imagination over form. Each artist searched for individual identity and expressed it in a personal way. If the artist was not better than others, he or she was at least different. Composers had great interest in literature and thought of themselves as "tone-poets"—expressing poetry in sounds, the universal language of music.

Romantic Traits

All periods have Romantic elements, but in the Romantic Period certain traits were dominant. The *majority* of artists:

- expressed an intense, almost mystical appreciation of nature.

- attempted to unify the arts (poets created visual arts, musicians wrote literary works and painters composed and performed music.)

- longed for the unobtainable.

- were fascinated with the past, dramatic medieval legends, the mystical and supernatural.

- showed interest in exotic lands and peoples.

- had a great interest in national identity.

Musical Style

Musical style comes through musicians as a result of their individual personalities and the characteristics of their time period. Musical style differs according to:

- **who** composed it.

- **where** it was written.

- **when** it was written.

- **why** it was written.

Forest (1866) by Renoir

*The painting to the right portrays the **Romantic mood** in the vastness and beauty of the landscape and in the image of the individual, deep in his own thoughts, surrounded by nature.*

© Planet Art

Carl Maria von Weber (1786–1826)

Carl Maria von Weber

Weber is one of the founders of Romanticism in music. A great virtuoso pianist of his day, he was known for his interpretations of Beethoven's sonatas. He introduced dramatic keyboard techniques in his music: tremolos, leaps from one register to another, arpeggios and other effects. He was a virtuoso on the guitar and a poet. A well-known music critic in his lifetime, he wrote on many aspects of music. His most famous works are his dramatic operas.

A brilliant conductor, to achieve better control, Weber was one of the first to stand in front of the orchestra (instead of conducting from the keyboard or violin). Recognizing the potential of each instrument, he wrote some of the most colorful orchestral music of all time.

WEBER LEADING HIS OPERA OF "DER FREISCHÜTZ" AT COVENT GARDEN THEATRE IN 1826.

Corbis-Bettmann

Weber in 1826, conducting his opera Der Freischütz *at Covent Garden Theatre in London, using a roll of paper as his baton.*

Weber's famous piano composition *Invitation to the Dance* and the *Waltz in C Major* (pages 12–13) have similar opening motives:

- ■ The program (or story line) opens with a melody in the bass clef, representing a man asking a woman to dance.

- ■ A melody in the treble clef follows, representing the woman's reply.

The *Waltz in C Major* also contains some keyboard techniques typical of Weber:

- ■ hand-crossings, register changes, dramatic dynamic changes and a melody accompanied by repeated chords.

---

[3]Geoffrey Skelton, transl., *Cosima Wagner Diaries,* Vol. 2 (London: Harcourt Brace Janovich, 1980), 914.

Waltz in C Major

Carl Maria von Weber
(1786–1826)

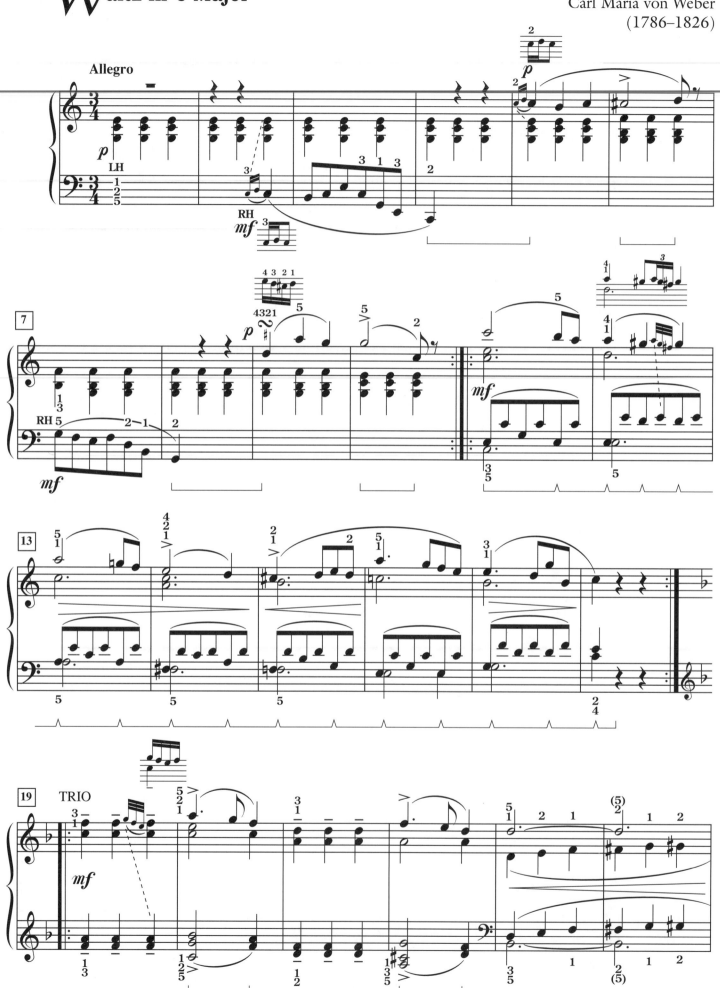

The Romantic Piano

The technology of the Industrial Revolution brought about the near completion of the modern piano by the mid-19th century.

Action from a Broadwood Grand Piano, 1799

The **single escapement** (sometimes nicknamed the "grasshopper") allows the hammer to fall away from the string while the key is still depressed.

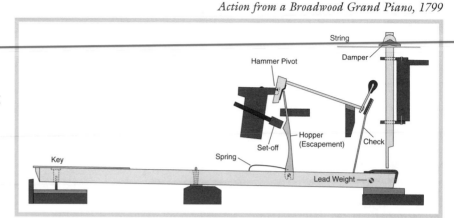

Érard's Double Escapement Action, 1822

The **double escapement** allows the hammer to fall partially while the key is depressed, and completely with the release of the key.

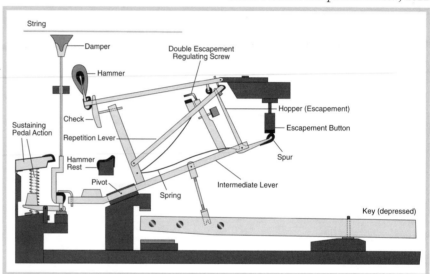

1794 Broadwood Grand Piano (similar to Beethoven's piano)

- The keyboard length was 5⅓ octaves.
- The wooden frame made it light in weight.
- Strings were thin, with a light tension.
- Hammers were light and leather covered.
- The single escapement action had limited response.

1857 Steinway Grand Piano (played by Liszt and Brahms)

- The keyboard length was 7⅓ octaves.
- The cast-iron frame made it heavy.
- Strings were thicker and covered with copper for greater strength.
- Hammers were larger, heavier and felt covered.
- The new double escapement action allowed faster repetition.

Franz Schubert (1797–1828)

"Truly in Schubert there is a divine spark."
Ludwig van Beethoven (1770–1827)[4]

Schubert lived his entire life in Vienna where he was best known as a composer of waltzes and other dances. He excelled in **miniatures** or small forms such as the **art song** (vocal settings of poems with the piano as an equal partner) and the **character piece** for solo piano.

Schubert never held an important musical position, achieved financial success or gained international fame during his lifetime. He was supported financially most of his life by friends, who were also artists.

He composed over 600 songs and was among the greatest art song composer of all time. Schubert died at the young age of 31. Of his over 1,000 works, few were published during his lifetime.

Viennese Soirées and Schubertiads

Middle-class Viennese families frequently held informal evenings of music-making by inviting friends to listen and participate in singing, dancing and playing instruments. Schubert and his friends also met regularly and were the most brilliant and interesting of Vienna's artists and intellectuals. Their parties became known as **Schubertiads**. Schubertiad entertainment:

- ◼ might include picnics, poetry readings, games of charades, acting out plays, playing ball games or discussing love and politics.

- ◼ always included dancing to music improvised at the piano by Schubert. The music was usually written down at a later time.

- ◼ always included Schubert performing his newest piano solos, duets and songs.

- ◼ became so well known that members of the aristocracy sometimes attended.

A Schubertiad, with Franz Schubert seated at the piano

AKG London

[4]John Amis and Michael Rose, eds., *Words About Music* (New York: Paragon House, 1992), 202.

This **transcription** (music written in one medium later arranged for another) for piano was originally one of Schubert's art songs.

*L*ob der Tränen *(Praise of Tears)*

Franz Schubert (1797–1828)
Arranged for piano by Louis Köhler (1820–1886)

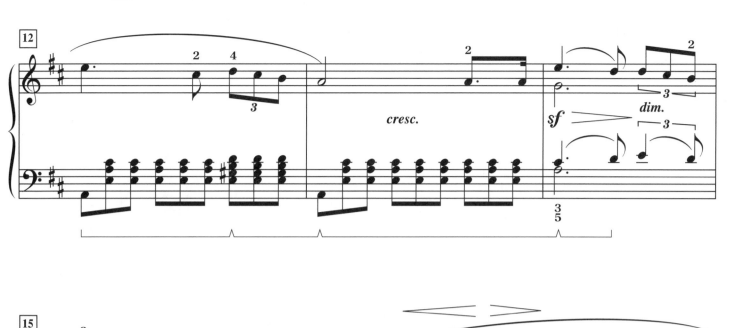

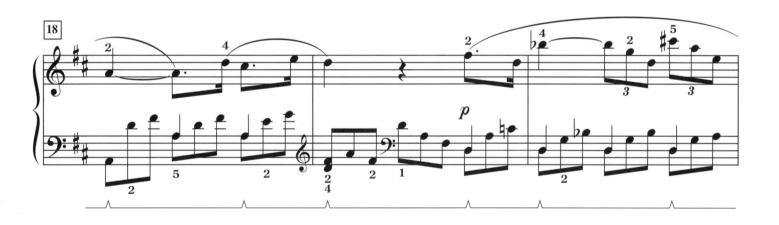

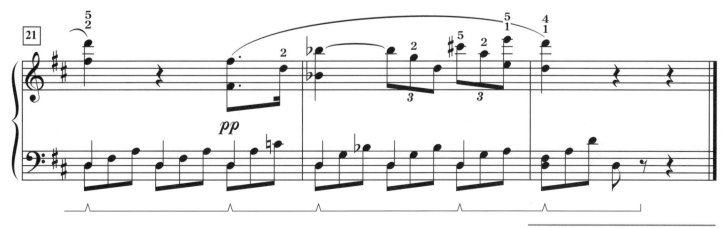

This *Moment Musical* is among Schubert's most famous piano pieces.
It was first published under the title *Russian Air*.

$\mathcal{M}$oment Musical

Franz Schubert (1797–1828)
Op. 94, No. 3

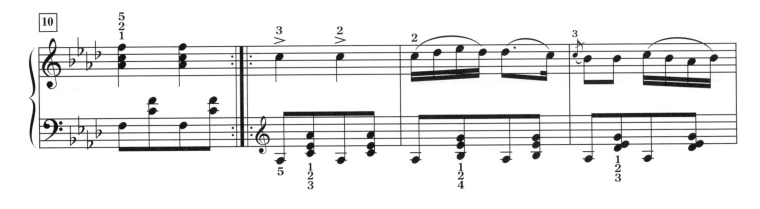

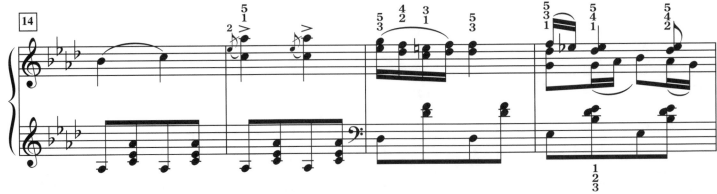

(a) The Editor suggests that grace notes be played before the beat.

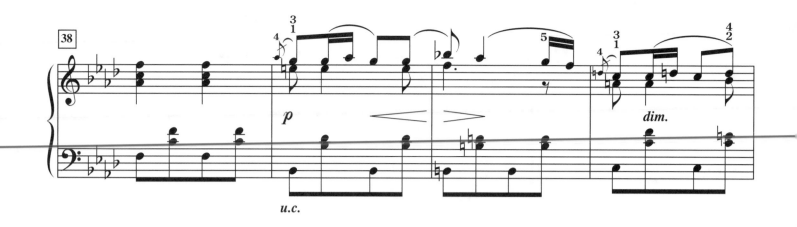

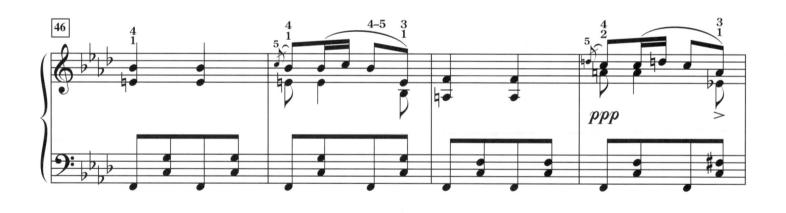

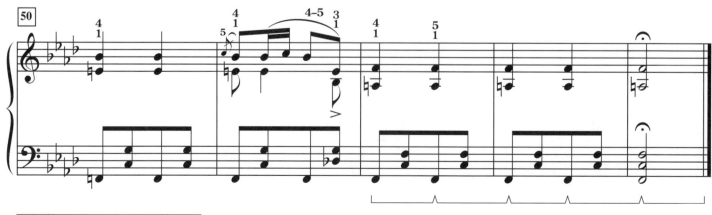

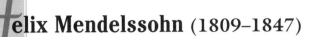

ℱelix Mendelssohn (1809–1847)

"I consider Mendelssohn to be the first musician of our time."
Robert Schumann (1810–1856)[5]

Felix Mendelssohn was a successful and well-respected musician in his own lifetime. Born into a wealthy family that appreciated and encouraged music, **his great natural musical gifts** were given every advantage of education and training. At a young age, he was famous as a pianist and organist, and was known to be a fine violinist as well. A musical genius, by age 17 he had written many compositions including the incidental music to Shakespeare's *A Midsummer Night's Dream.*

He composed all musical forms: symphonies, concertos, cantatas, chamber music, oratorios, operas and incidental music, songs, and solo pieces for both piano and organ.

Mendelssohn was also a writer, poet, musicologist, linguist, and a professional water colorist and landscape artist.

© Planet Art

Felix Mendelssohn

As a **pianist, composer** and **conductor,** he toured Germany, Austria, France, Italy, Scotland and Switzerland, and made 10 visits to England where Queen Victoria (1819–1901) was one of his greatest admirers. He founded and directed the Leipzig Conservatory and taught piano and composition there.

As a **conductor**, he:

- ▣ improved orchestral performance standards.

- ▣ introduced and supported young artists, such as Clara Schumann (1819–1896).

- ▣ revived historical repertoire including the first performance of Schubert's *Symphony No. 9 in C Major* ("Great") and the first presentation in almost 100 years of J. S. Bach's (1685–1750) *St. Matthew Passion.*

The Mendelssohn Family Salon in Berlin

Theatrical performances, literary readings and regular Sunday musicales made the Mendelssohn home a **center of musical and intellectual thought,** and the most important salon in Berlin. An orchestra was hired to perform Felix's compositions and for him to conduct. Other family members, like his sister Fanny [Hensel] (1805–1847), and visiting artists also performed. Guests included scientists, philosophers, diplomats, theologians, historians, linguists, poets, nobles, critics, professional actors and musicians—leaders of European intellectual and social life.

[5]Heinrich Jacob, *Felix Mendelssohn and His Times,* trans. Richard and Clara Winston (Englewood Cliffs, NJ: Prentice-Hall, 1963), 98.

This piece shows the new style Mendelssohn created in many of his 48 *Songs without Words*, which were intended for performance in parlors and drawing rooms. This new style has both a **songlike theme** and **instrumental accompaniment.**

Andante sostenuto

Felix Mendelssohn (1809–1847)
Op. 72, No. 2

ⓐ The Editor suggests that grace notes be played before the beat.

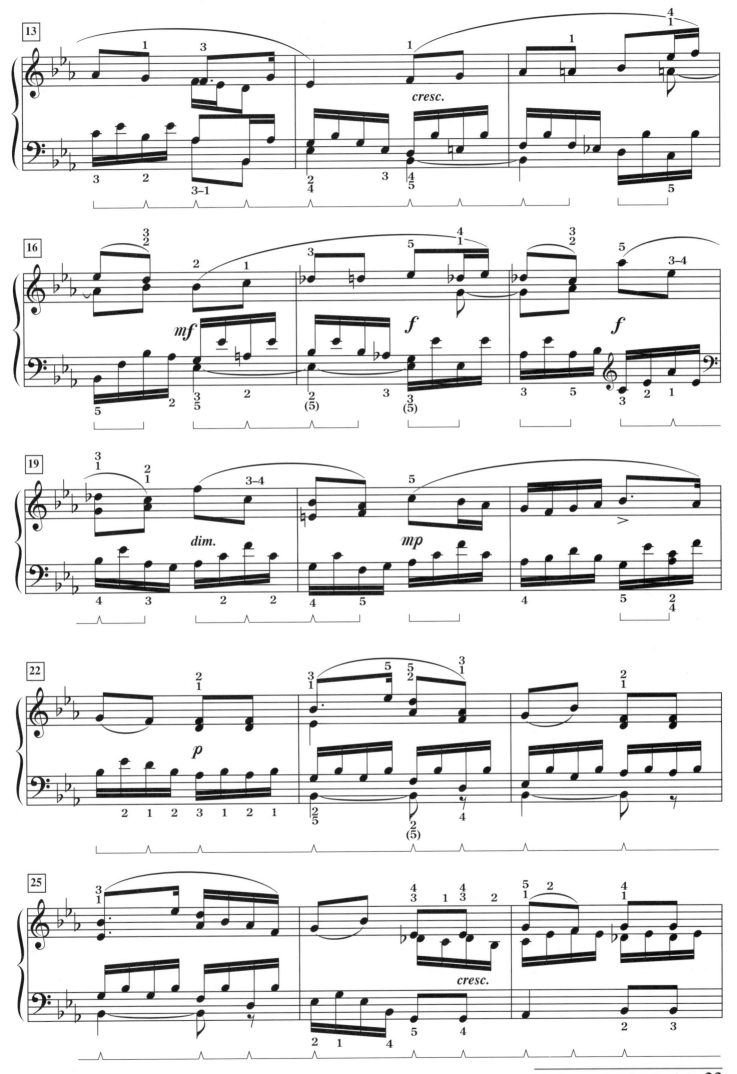

Niels Gade (1817–1890)

Gade was a Danish composer, conductor and violinist. His *Symphony No. 1 in C Minor,* *Op. 5* was premiered in Germany with Felix Mendelssohn conducting. Later Mendelssohn appointed Gade to the Leipzig Conservatory faculty. In 1848, when war broke out between Prussia and Denmark, Gade returned to Copenhagen where he had great influence on Danish musical life.

Boy's Round Dance

Niels Gade (1817–1890)
Op. 36, No. 3B

Allegro vivace

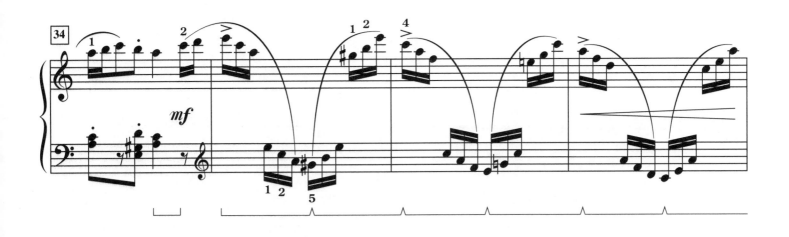

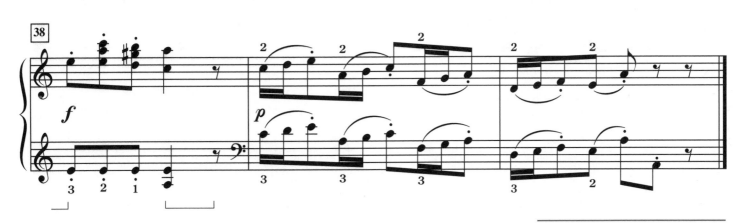

"Music is to me the perfect expression of the soul."
Robert Schumann[6]

Robert Schumann (1810–1856)

Robert Schumann

Schumann is sometimes called the most Romantic of all composers.

- He used literary, nonmusical associations in his music.

- His **miniatures,** or short piano pieces and songs, are among his best works.

- His music is personal, even autobiographical, in expression.

- His personality was introspective; his style was lyric or melodic.

Robert's mother insisted he study law at Leipzig University. Most of his time there was spent in musical activities, including piano study with the famous German piano teacher Friedrich Wieck (1785–1873).

Robert fell deeply in love with Friedrich's talented daughter Clara Wieck (1819–1896). Known as the 19th-century "queen of the piano," she had begun her career as a concert pianist at age 12. After several years of bitter legal battles with her father, Robert and Clara were finally married.

A mechanical device that Robert designed to strengthen his fourth finger destroyed it, along with his career as a concert pianist. He then focused on composing music and writing about it. He struggled with mental illness most of his life; after a suicide attempt, his final years were spent in an asylum.

Robert and his wife Clara. A well-known concert pianist, Clara played Robert's music and made it known throughout Europe after his death.

[6]Joseph Machlis, *The Enjoyment of Music* (New York: W. W. Norton, 1977), 79.

His Musical Compositions

Mainly self-taught, he composed in all forms. He developed the Romantic **piano suite** or **cycle**—short piano works, loosely linked. The cycles, connected through a title, theme or idea, show emotional contrasts in the pieces.

- His music was considered too dissonant for the average listener of his day.

- He was one of the first to indicate extensive use of the damper pedal in his piano music.

His Literary Writings

In his lifetime, he was known more as a music critic than as a composer. For 10 years he edited a newspaper that commented on new music.

- Through his writings he supported music of quality and young talented artists, trying to "dam up the tide of mediocrity."

- He wrote under **pen names** that expressed his dual personality and nature. *Florestan* was the passionate hero. *Eusebius* was the poetic dreamer. *Raro* (ClaRA-RObert) was a blend of the two personalities.

This piece is an example of Schumann's use of **hidden musical codes** since the notes of the theme spell G-A-D-E. Niels Gade was the assistant conductor to Mendelssohn of the Gewandhaus Orchestra, and became the principal conductor after Mendelssohn's death. Gade and Schumann became friends while teaching at the Leipzig Conservatory. When Gade left Leipzig to return to Denmark, Schumann composed this piece.

Northern Song (Greeting to G)

Robert Schumann (1810–1856)
Op. 68, No. 41

This piece is from *Carnaval*, a set of 21 short pieces describing a masked ball.

- ▣ The individual pieces are mood pictures, and describe characters and events.
- ▣ Guests depicted at the imaginary ball make it a musical picture gallery. Schumann himself, Clara, Friedrich Wieck (1785–1873), Niccolò Paganini (1782–1840), Felix Mendelssohn (1809–1847) and Frédéric Chopin (1810–1849) are all present. This tribute is a **Chopin-like nocturne.**

Chopin *from Carnaval, Op. 9*

Robert Schumann (1810–1856)

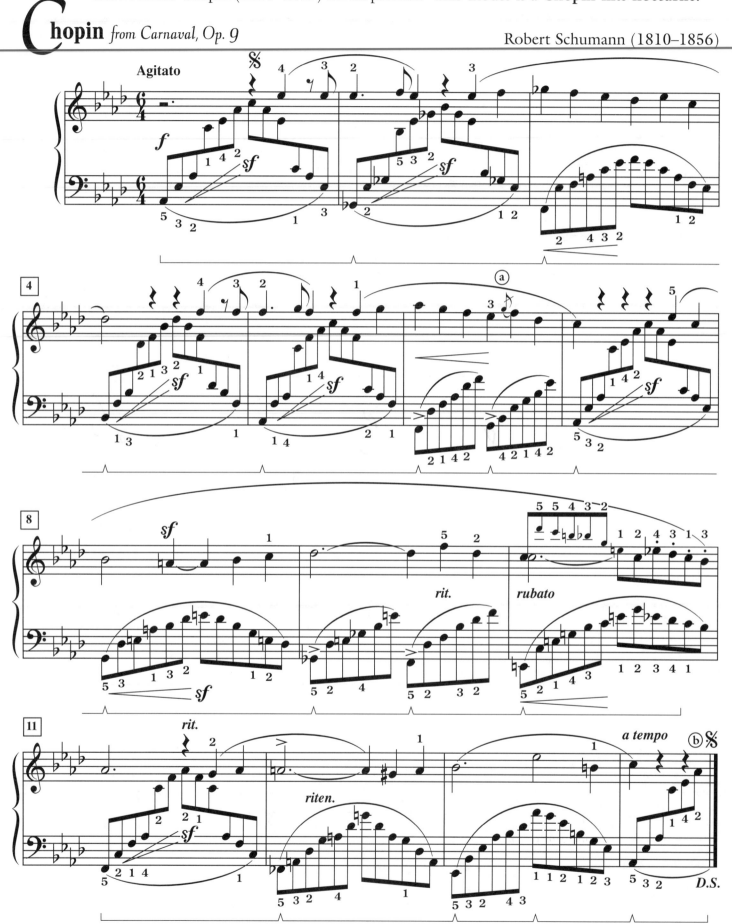

ⓐ The Editor suggests that the grace note be played before the beat.

ⓑ This piece contains no ending. The Editor suggests to end after one repeat.

Frédéric François Chopin (1810–1849)

"Hats off, gentlemen! A genius!"
Robert Schumann on Chopin[7]

Born in Poland, **Chopin** began his career playing piano concerts in aristocratic homes and palaces in Warsaw at age 8. On tour in Vienna at age 20, he learned that Warsaw had been captured by Russia, and he settled permanently in Paris.

His debut concert in Paris, attended by Franz Liszt (1811–1886) and Felix Mendelssohn (1809–1847), established him as a composer and piano virtuoso. He played only about 30 public concerts in his lifetime, preferring intimate salons.

His main income was from publishing and teaching society ladies. After several years of illness, he died of tuberculosis at age 39. Although he never returned to Poland, his music became a symbol of Polish freedom, even during World War II.

Chopin in the salon of the Prince Anton Radziwill

© AKG Photo, London

Chopin and Parisian Salons

From about 1830 to 1850, Paris was the intellectual and artistic center of world. The intellects of the day (writers, artists, ambassadors, princes, ministers) met in each other's homes to discuss issues, exchange ideas, be entertained and be seen.

Paris became the headquarters of European pianists. The German poet, writer and journalist Heinrich Heine (1797–1856) said, "Like locusts, the pianists invade Paris every winter ... to make a name for themselves here, from which they can then profit ... in other countries."[8]

Franz Liszt described the guests at the salon of the music publisher and piano manufacturer Ignaz Joseph Pleyel (1757–1831) as "the most elegant ladies, the most famous artists, the richest financiers, the most illustrious lords ... a complete aristocracy of birth, wealth, talent and beauty."[9] Novelist and Chopin's companion George Sand (1804–1876) said that Chopin could choose from between 20 and 30 salons to visit on any evening.

[7]Dominic Gill, ed., *The Book of the Piano* (Ithaca, NY: Cornell University Press, 1981), 80.
[8]*Color Library Book of Great Composers* (London: Marshall Cavendish, 1989), 162.
[9]Ibid., 16.

Chopin is the only major composer who wrote almost exclusively piano music. Because of mechanical improvements, especially in hammer quality, the piano of his day was capable of greater tonal and dynamic range. Chopin wrote for the instrument in new ways, showing its full potential.

This piece is an example of his **cantabile** or **singing style**. The melody is accompanied by widely spaced chords in the bass, sustained by the damper pedal.

Cantabile

Frédéric François Chopin
(1810–1849)

ⓐ The Editor suggests that the grace note be played before the beat.

The **mazurka** was a Polish folk song and country dance originating near Warsaw.
A few of Chopin's mazurkas are intended for dancing, but he had taken their **national characteristics** (rhythms and spirit) and transferred them to a concert setting. Some of Chopin's mazurkas have no definite endings (like this one), leaving the impression that the music disappears into the air.

"Endless" Mazurka

Frédéric François Chopin (1810–1849)
Op. 7, No. 5

ⓐ If the performer wishes, after playing the desired number of repeats, the piece could end in m. 12 as shown.

Cécile Chaminade
(1857–1944)

At age 8, the French composer **Cécile Chaminade's** church music was praised by opera composer Georges Bizet (1838–1875), who predicted a brilliant future for her. She became a successful solo pianist and conductor. Her compositions include songs, chamber music, ballet, orchestral pieces, an opera and over 200 piano pieces.

Élégies were originally poems, frequently mourning a death. This musical élégie has a singing melody over a flowing, "blended" accompaniment.

Élégie

Cécile Chaminade (1857–1944)
Op. 126, No. 7

ⓐ The Editor suggests that grace notes be played before the beat.

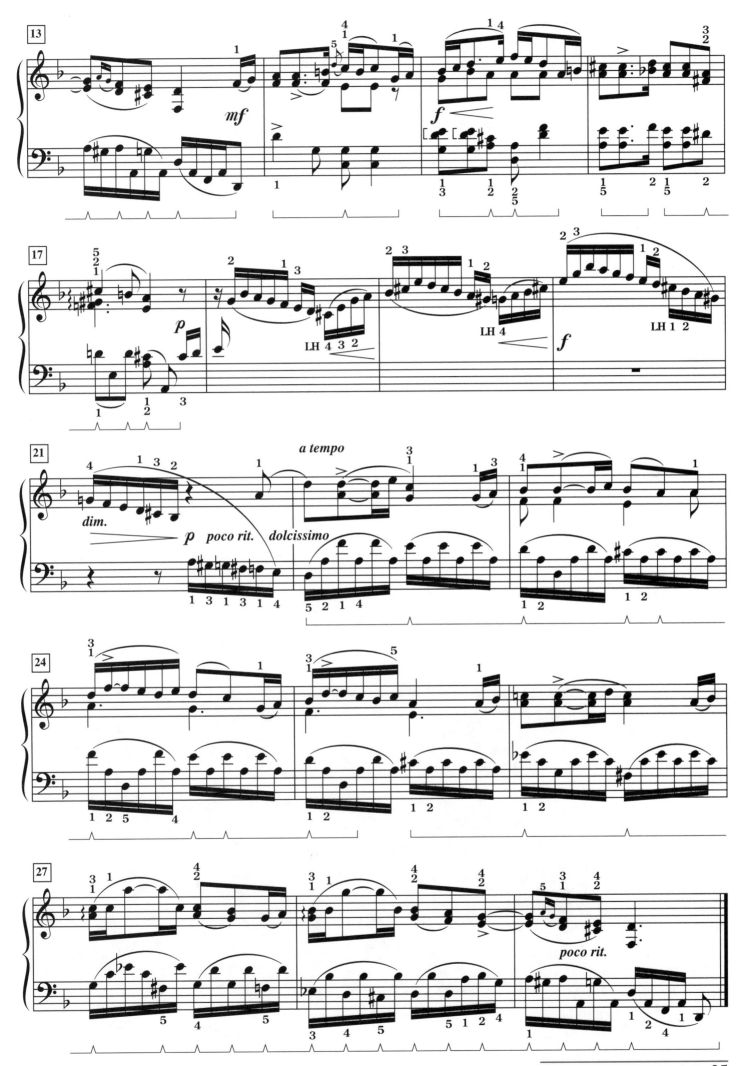

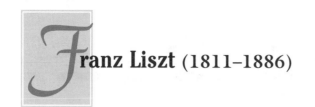

Franz Liszt (1811–1886)

Liszt, the Ultimate Romantic

In addition to being a renowned composer, Liszt was also a conductor, teacher, editor, critic, writer, philosopher and philanthropist, and one of the greatest pianists of his time, perhaps of all time. He was born in Hungary on the Esterházy estate (Prince Nikolaus Esterházy was the patron of Franz Joseph Haydn), where his father was a servant to the Prince and an amateur musician.

Liszt studied piano and composition briefly, but was largely self-taught and self-educated. He composed over 400 piano pieces, which expanded the technical possibilities of the instrument. For orchestra, he created the **symphonic poem,** a one-movement programmatic work inspired by literature or art.

- Liszt settled in Paris where he became friends with Hector Berlioz (1803–1869), Frédéric François Chopin (1810–1849) and other artists of the day.

- He was a literary man who wrote articles supporting and explaining the music of Chopin, Berlioz, Richard Wagner (1813–1883) and other "moderns."

- Playing many benefit concerts to raise money for worthy causes, he helped many composers and performers artistically and financially.

- Liszt's extraordinary pianism changed the status of musicians from servant to favored celebrity. He brought piano music out of middle-class homes into the concert hall.

- At age 36, Liszt gave up touring as a pianist and became Music Director for the Court in Weimar, Germany where he conducted and promoted new music.

- Pianists came from everywhere to study with him, so his teaching influenced pianists and teachers throughout the world.

L. Bösendorfer Klavier fabrik GmbH

Liszt playing a Bösendorfer for the Emperor Franz Josef of Austria

[10]Harold C. Schonberg, *The Virtuosi* (New York: Random House, 1988), 126.

From left to right, Liszt's daughter, Cosima; his son-in-law, Richard Wagner; and Franz Liszt, in his old age.

"Whoever has not heard Liszt cannot even speak of piano playing."
Johannes Brahms[11]

Liszt, the Piano Virtuoso

When he was 10, a review of Liszt said, "A virtuoso has dropped from the clouds. There is a god amongst us."[12] When he was 12, a Paris review said, "His feet can hardly touch the pedals … yet he is the first pianist in Europe."[13]

His piano technique was called **transcendental**, beyond human possibility. He made the piano sound like an orchestra with his dynamic extremes and huge sonorities.

He invented the **solo piano recital,** an entire evening of piano music played by himself. Audiences were thrilled by his magnetic personality, skill and passion. As the first "superstar," he encouraged "Lisztomania" by occasionally collapsing into the arms of his page turner before being carried off stage. Ladies screamed, wept, fainted from excitement and threw bouquets onto the stage. Two Hungarian countesses once fought on the floor over his snuffbox.

He composed and performed many **transcriptions,** or arrangements of famous songs and themes, like Mendelssohn's art song, *On Wings of Song* (pages 38–40). One crowd-pleasing technique used in this piece is the **three hands trick**, where the melody is played with alternate thumbs, while harmonic lines swirl above and below it.

[11]Derek Watson, ed. introduction and selection, *Dictionary of Musical Quotations* (Ware Hertfordshire: Cumberland House, Wordsworth Editions Ltd., 1994), 247.

[12]*Color Library,* 183.

[13]Ibid., 183.

On Wings of Song ⓐ

Felix Mendelssohn (1809–1847)
Arranged for piano by Franz Liszt (1811–1886)

ⓐ This Liszt transcription has been abbreviated by the Editor to include only the first statement of the song.

ⓑ The Editor suggests first playing the melody (middle line) alone with the designated hands and fingers.
Play the downstem melody notes with the left hand and the upstem notes with the right hand.

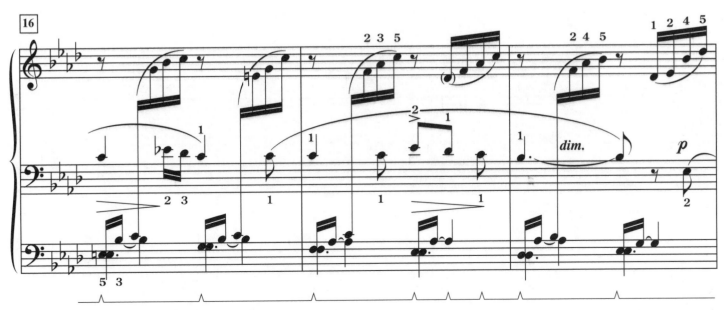

ⓒ The Editor suggests that grace notes be played before the beat.

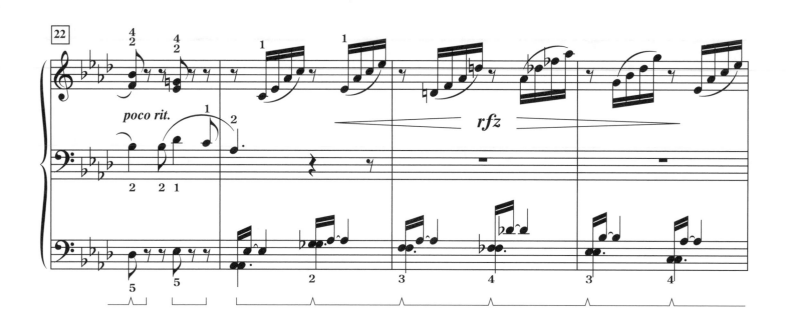

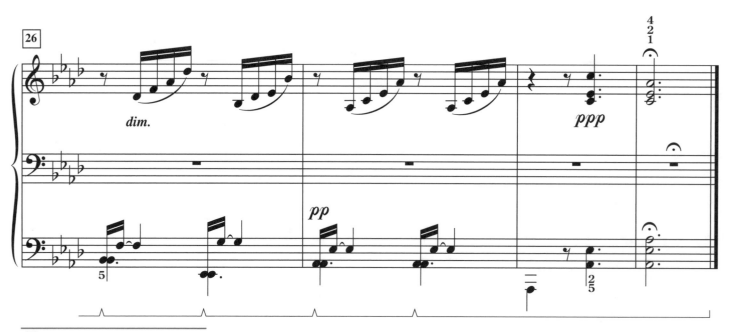

*"Oh, how difficult it is to make anyone see
and feel in music what we see and feel ourselves!"*
Tchaikovsky[14]

Peter Ilyich Tchaikovsky (1840–1893)

Tchaikovsky remains one of the most famous Russian composers. In contrast to his fame and brilliant career, he was an incredibly shy and melancholy person. He said, "Every new meeting with someone unknown has always been for me a source of suffering."[15]

He was a brilliant child who could read French and German by age 6, and could write French poetry by age 7. He also began piano lessons at this time and was soon better than his teacher, yet he never became a virtuoso. After studying law, Tchaikovsky became a clerk in the Ministry of Justice, keeping music as a hobby. At age 21, he began studying music seriously at the St. Petersburg Conservatory, and soon resigned his civil servant position to become a full-time music student. Anton Rubinstein (1829–1894), noted pianist and Tchaikovsky's composition teacher, recommended that Tchaikovsky teach harmony at the newly founded Moscow Conservatory.

Tchaikovsky's **ballets** (*The Nutcracker; Swan Lake*) and **orchestral music** (*Overture to Romeo and Juliet; 1812 Overture;* six symphonies) brought him international fame. He toured western Europe as a conductor. In 1891, he conducted his *Concerto in B-flat Minor for Piano* during opening week of Carnegie Hall in New York City, where he was quoted, "I am 10 times more famous here than in Europe."[16]

His soaring melodies, richly orchestrated scores and heartfelt emotion have made him one of most frequently performed and best-loved composers in the world.

Corbis-Bettmann

Tchaikovsky sitting in the garden of his country home in Klin where he lived as a near hermit. This is now the Tchaikovsky State Museum.

[14]Watson, *Music Quotations*, 98.

[15]Harold C. Schonberg, *Lives of the Great Composers* (New York: Norton, 1981), 378.

[16]Elsa Z. Posell, *Russian Composers* (Boston: Houghton Mifflin, 1967), 69.

Although trained in the techniques of Western music, Tchaikovsky frequently used Russian folk and dance tunes in his music. The repetition of these motives builds emotional intensity in the piece.

Russian Dance

Peter Ilyich Tchaikovsky (1840–1893)
Op. 40, No. 10

(a) The Editor suggests that grace notes be played before the beat.

Allegro molto vivace

Johannes Brahms (1833–1897)

Brahms composed masterpieces in every form of music except opera. Showing ability in music at a young age, he contributed to the family income by playing piano in taverns and arranging music for publication. He also wrote serious compositions for piano and voice at this time.

At the age of 20, Brahms was invited to accompany a violinist on tour where he met prominent musicians Franz Liszt, and Clara and Robert Schumann, who were shown his compositions. He lived with the Schumanns for several months, and was of great support to Clara during the two years Robert was institutionalized. He and Clara had a deep 40-year friendship.

- Settling in Vienna, he held conducting positions where he performed his own music and that of earlier, especially Baroque, composers.

- Although he had a shy, abrupt personality, he was also humble and generous, and helped many young musicians with their careers.

- He was one of the first to do scholarly research and editing of music.

- Well known as a composer throughout Europe, he lived comfortably on earnings from his concerts and publications.

Brahms's Musical Style

Brahms continued the German tradition of **J. S. Bach** (independent voices) and **Beethoven** (development of motives). They are sometimes linked as **"The Three 'B's."** Rather than program music, he wrote fugues, variations, chamber music and symphonies, bringing Romantic expression and harmonies to existing classical forms. Almost every work he composed is still performed today.

- His complex yet subtle rhythms are unique.

- His thick textures create full, rich piano sounds.

- Arpeggios become melodic phrases, not mere accompaniment.

- The mood created in his expressive melodies and harmonies is deeply felt within only a few measures.

Brahms as an accompanist in the Bösendorfer Hall in Vienna

AKG London

[17]Dieter Hildebrandt, *Pianoforte* (New York: George Braziller, Inc., 1990), 130.

Brahms's first and last compositions were piano solos, the last ones being short **character pieces**. His later piano pieces (Op. 76 through 119) are among the greatest in the piano literature. Common titles are **capriccio** and **intermezzo**, the latter being slower and more reflective.

Intermezzo in A Minor

Johannes Brahms (1833–1897)
Op. 76, No. 7

This **waltz,** from his Op. 39 set of 16 waltzes, is one of Brahms's most famous pieces.

altz in A-flat Major

Johannes Brahms (1833–1897)
Op. 39, No. 15

Teneramente e grazioso

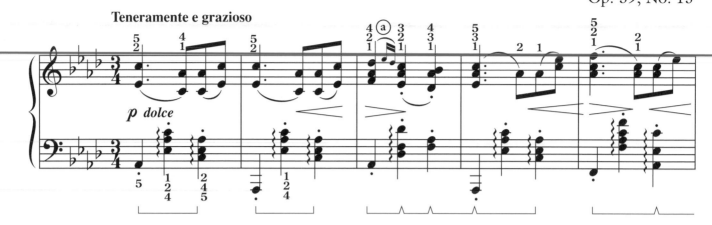

(a) The Editor suggests that grace notes be played before the beat.

![E]dward MacDowell (1860–1908)

MacDowell was one of the first American composers to gain international recognition. His inspiration came more from the beauty and majesty of nature than from American folk elements. He was born in New York City and taken to Paris to study music at age 15. While a student at the Paris Conservatory, he also was offered a scholarship to study painting, but refused it to focus on piano and composition.

Edward and Marian MacDowell

- After studying in Paris for a year, MacDowell decided to continue his studies in Germany. He was so successful that when he graduated, at age 21, he was appointed to the piano faculty of the Darmstadt Conservatory.

- In 1881, he visited Franz Liszt (1811–1886) at Weimar and played his *Piano Concerto No. 1 in A Minor* for him. Liszt invited him to perform in a concert with other composers in Zurich, and recommended his works to the leading German publisher, Breitkopf & Härtel, who published several of his compositions. MacDowell thought of himself as a composer who performed, rather than as a concert pianist.

- In 1888 he returned to the United States, settling in Boston where he taught, performed and composed. In 1896 he became the first Chairman of the new music department at Columbia University. His *Piano Concerto No. 2 in D Minor* established him in the United States, and is still performed today.

- He died from a mental illness, worsened by a horse-cab accident.

The MacDowell Artists' Colony

- In 1896 the MacDowells bought property near Peterborough, New Hampshire, where he could compose in peace. He had a log cabin built in the woods away from the main house, for even greater privacy.

- In 1906 Edward decided to invite other artists to work there, and exchange ideas.

- After his death Mrs. MacDowell raised money for expansion, and managed the artists' colony.

- Today over 1,000 composers, writers and visual artists apply annually for residencies lasting from two weeks to three months; about 200 are chosen.

- Former residents include American composers Leonard Bernstein (1918–1990), Aaron Copland (1900–1990), Samuel Barber (1910–1981), Norman Dello Joio (b. 1913), and poet Robert Frost (1874–1963).

The cabin where MacDowell composed

(From "A Log Cabin")
A house of dreams untold,
It looks out over the whispering tree-tops
And faces the setting sun.

Edward MacDowell[18]

---

[18]Edward MacDowell, *New England Idyls*, Op. 62 (Boston: Arthur P. Schmidt, 1902), 24.

MacDowell wrote over 100 **character pieces** for piano, which are considered to be among his best works. Similar in style to the **lyric pieces** of Norwegian composer and pianist Edvard Grieg (1843–1907), many of MacDowell's works were inspired by nature. MacDowell wrote that his descriptive music "[was] not written with the idea of describing the thing itself, but [was written to create] the atmosphere surrounding it."[19]

After his death, his wife played many concerts featuring his music, helping popularize it.

The Brook

Edward MacDowell (1860–1908)
Op. 32, No. 2

[19]Grace Overmyer, *Famous American Composers* (New York: Thomas Y. Crowell Co., 1945), 122.

ⓐ The Editor suggests that grace notes be played before the beat.

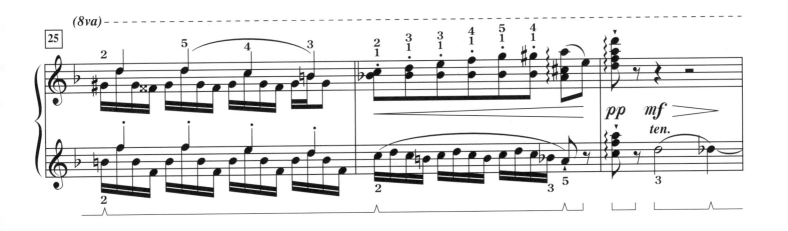

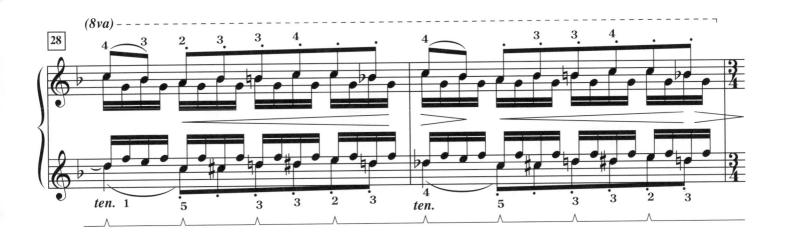

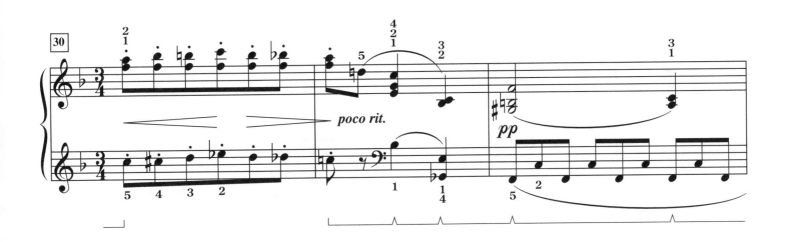

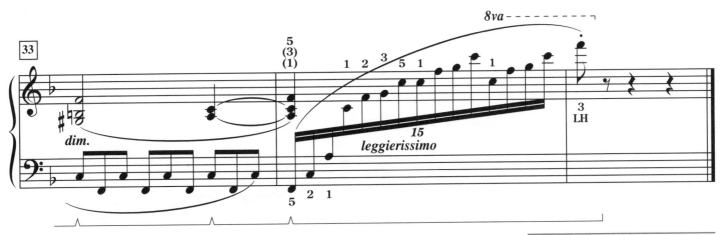

This piece is from a set entitled *Forgotten Fairy Tales.* MacDowell published the set under the pseudonym of Edgar Thorn.

Sung Outside the Prince's Door

Edward MacDowell (1860–1908)
Op. 4, No. 1

(a) If necessary, break this chord, playing the lower note ahead of the beat. Catch the lower note with the damper pedal.

Edvard Grieg (1843–1907)

"The Chopin of the North."
German pianist and conductor
Hans von Bülow (1830–1894) on Grieg[20]

Grieg, one of the greatest Norwegian composers, was also a conductor, writer and pianist. Born into a musical family, he performed in regular musical gatherings held in their home. He composed and performed well on the piano by age 15, and was sent to study at the Leipzig Conservatory, where his teachers were Louis Plaidy (1810–1874), Ignaz Moscheles (1794–1870) and Carl Reinecke (1824–1910). He later went to Copenhagen and was encouraged and advised by Niels Gade (1817–1890).

A close friend, Rikard Nordraak (1842–1866), collected Norwegian folk songs, and together they developed a distinct Norwegian musical style. Norwegian folk melodies, rhythms and harmonies did become prominent in Grieg's music. His use of **folk elements** created a unique musical style that has had lasting appeal.

He performed in many recitals throughout Europe as a soloist and with his wife Nina, a professional singer, who sang his songs and played piano duets with him. In Rome, Franz Liszt played his *Piano Concerto in A Minor,* Op. 16, at sight, and encouraged him. Later Grieg supported and encouraged composers worldwide, such as Jean Sibelius (Finnish, 1865–1957), Carl Nielsen (Danish, 1865–1931), Frederick Delius (English, 1862–1934) and Percy Grainger (Austrailian-born American, 1882–1961).

Grieg's music became popular and well known throughout Europe, and he was awarded numerous honors from different countries. His most famous work is the incidental music for Henrik Ibsen's (1828–1906) play *Peer Gynt,* yet his best compositions are in **miniatures**; over 140 art songs and over 100 short piano pieces.

"My wife ... has been ... the only genuine interpreter of my songs."
Edvard Grieg[21]

Nationalmuseum Stockholm

Portrait of Edvard Grieg accompanying his wife Nina, by P. S. Krøer

---

[20]Milton Cross and David Ewen, *The Milton Cross New Encyclopedia of the Great Composers and Their Music,* Vol. 1 (Garden City, NY: Doubleday & Company, Inc., 1969), 405.

[21]Stanley Sadie, ed., *The New Grove Dictionary of Music and Musicians,* Vol. 7 (New York: Macmillan, 1980), 717.

Inspired by nature and love of his country, for several years Grieg composed from the solitude of a hut that overlooked Norway's Hardanger Fjord. The entire Op. 17 consists of piano solo arrangements of **Norwegian folk songs** and **folk dances**.

Ole's Song

Edvard Grieg (1843–1907)
Op. 17, No. 10

Grieg first wrote this as a piano duet, and later arranged it for piano solo.

Norwegian Dance

Edvard Grieg (1843–1907)
Op. 35, No. 2

ⓐ The Editor suggests that grace notes be played before the beat.

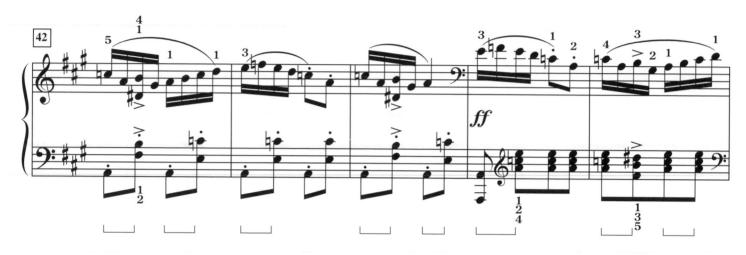

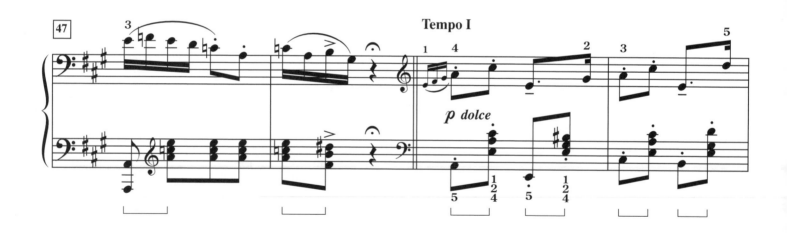

Grieg said the folk music he used came from a time when Norwegian peasants were isolated
from the world in solitary mountain-valleys; when young boys watched over cows in a pasture.

Song of the Cowherd

Edvard Grieg (1843–1907)
Op. 17, No. 22

Andante con moto